VIDEO SCRIPT WRITING

How to Write Better Scripts for Your Digital Video

© 2015 Jonathan Halls. All rights reserved.

Published by Talkshow Media LLC. PO Box 248 Clifton, VA 20124, USA.

ISBN 13 - 9781514717622

No part of this publication may be reproduced in any way without express permission from the publisher. This includes storage for a retrieval system or transmission in any form other than that agreed to by the publisher, in any form or means which includes electronic, mechanical, photocopying recording or otherwise. Individual quotes of up to one paragraph are allowed subject to referencing the author.

CONTENTS AT A GLANCE

INTRODUCTION — 4
How This Book Can Help You

PART ONE — 14
Media Communication Basics

- Sensory Register — 21
- Working Memory — 21
- Long-Term Memory — 22
- Implications for Video Writers — 23

PART TWO — 28
Video Psychology

- Message Layers — 31

PART THREE — 36
Video Scripts

- Why write a Script? — 38
- Spoken Word in Video — 40
- Principles of Writing Video Scripts — 41
- Script Layout — 44

PART FOUR — 48
The Practice of Writing Video Scripts

- Writing Your Script — 50
- Sentences — 54
- Words — 62

INTRODUCTION

How This Book Can Help You

INTRODUCTION

VIDEO SCRIPTS

Today everyone is a broadcaster, publisher and producer. In fact, most of us carry television cameras around in our pockets – our cell phones.

But not everyone produces video that's engaging to a broad number of people. That's OK for some types of video. If it's a sequence of shaky-cam shots from your Caribbean holiday or the memorable first steps of your youngest child, it doesn't really matter.

However, if you're creating deliberate content such as a product demo, inspirational message or training video, you can't leave it to chance. Winging

HOW THIS BOOK CAN HELP YOU

One chance many videographers take is not writing a script. Rather than plan the spoken word elements of their video, they improvise, adlibbing voice overs and monologues. Sometimes it turns out OK. But you can't wing it all the time and expect to deliver a consistently high impact.

Video Scripts are an Investment

Whether you're making video for a corporate communications department, small business, training division, church or local community organization, writing a script is a good investment. Well-written scripts make your video look better, they focus your message, keep it consistent and save time and money.

Of course, simply writing a script is not going to guarantee good video. You need to write it well. That involves following a set of writing rules most of us were not taught at school. At school we were taught to write for the eye – people read your words. People hear your words in video so the rules are different.

it is complacent at best, reckless at its worst. Every minute of good web video will take you anything from two to five hours to produce. The more you wing it, the more time you waste and the higher the risk you take that your video will have no impact.

INTRODUCTION

I've written this book to help you explore what this means so you can write great video scripts. I know people are busy these days so I've tried my best to write a book that's less than a hundred pages to make it a quick read. We've also adopted a layout style that is influenced by magazine design so you can flip through the book as much as read it from beginning to end.

Good luck with your video.

Jonathan Halls
Washington, DC 2015.

RAPID MEDIA TECHNIQUE

Producing Video Fast Without Compromising Quality

I've taught media to thousands of people around the world working in newspapers, radio stations, TV stations and digital media. The first nineteen years of my media training career were spent working across the world exclusively with folks in the media biz like journalists, writers and producers.

However, since moving to the United States six years ago, I have increasingly worked with non-media folks finding their role in today's world where everyone is a broadcaster, publisher and producer. It's gratifying to see people find new and more powerful ways to communicate that were, until just a few years ago, out of reach to anyone but a privileged few who had jobs in professional media.

Rapid Media Technique (Video)

1. Identify purpose
2. Determine video is appropriate
3. Break into chunks
4. Arrange into a pattern
5. Draw storyboard
6. Write script
7. Create production plan
8. Shoot video
9. Edit video
10. Distribute

Workflow & Habit

Over the years I have learned that in order to consistently churn out quality content, you need to have an effective workflow. Even though top producers make their content look fresh and spontaneous, they never leave things to chance. The most inspiring media experts and productive media organizations I've worked with over the past 25 years all had highly effective routines for churning out top content.

However, having good routines or workflows is not enough. These need to be ingrained so everyone in your team follows them. This helps them work faster and more creatively.

I've watched and helped a lot of folks who struggle to make engaging digital content. Significantly, most of them have ineffective workflows. Some don't even have a workflow and do things differently every time they make a video. They forget some tasks, confuse others and find themselves unpicking half-hearted work.

To help my clients and provide a rigorous structure for the seminars I teach around the world, I developed a workflow to demystify the production process and help people learn digital production faster.

RMT Emphasizes Planning

I call this workflow the Rapid Media Technique. RMT for short. And I have an RMT for video, audio and web writing. Of course, there are many ways to approach production efficiently. The RMT workflow does not suggest other approaches are better or worse. Rather, this is a workflow I have seen help many of my clients and students. I base all my workshops and seminars on this technique because it gets results and quickly helps people learn the craft of digital content. It also provides a foundation for building good habits. This book is written within the context of RMT.

RMT places an emphasis on planning. We start with one clearly defined purpose then determine if the topic is suitable for video. (If the topic is not visual or could easily survive as an audio podcast, video is not the best option.) Then we break the purpose down into knowledge chunks and create a narrative structure. At this point, we take the narrative structure and turn it into a storyboard. Notice how we haven't even written a script and we're half-way through the process? An important principle of RMT is to draw the storyboard before writing the script. Once you have written your script you create a production plan, shoot the video and edit it.

The idea of writing a script after drawing a storyboard is counterintuitive for many people. They assume you start with the script then search for visual ideas. But as we discuss later, "script before pictures" makes less conceptual sense. And at a practical level, writing your script after the storyboard saves time and results in better pictures.

Why I wrote this Book

I teach RMT in my two-day classes and one-day video boot camps. Both are packed and intense, but the reality is we can't cover everything in just a few days. We cover the foundations on which you can build. Becuase time is money and we understand how tough it is to be out of the office, we keep the classes to two days. As a consequence of this, I get a lot of follow-up emails

INTRODUCTION

asking for additional resources to learn more about the foundational topics we cover.

This book was prompted by one such email. A communications professional in Nebraska, who attended one of my workshops in Las Vegas, emailed for more resources on script writing. I've had a lot of requests about how to write a great script. So this book is a product of what he and a bunch of other people keep asking me for. I expect this will be the first in a series of short books to deepen their resources.

Is This Book for You?

As you determine if this book will be of value to you, I want to be clear that I am writing about short, factual video – the type of digital content people will watch on YouTube, in a learning management system or video sharing site. It could be a documentary about safety in your organization. Or a how to video of "Basic Yoga Moves" to promote your local wellness studio on YouTube. We're not looking at screenwriting or writing a TV soap opera.

This book is very deliberately focused on the mechanics and language of writing your script.

To meet my aim of writing a short book, I have worked hard to avoid the temptation of branching off into other related areas of video creation such as video structure and narrative, or drawing storyboards and associated topics of shot sizes and so forth. I have focused rather on the script writing stage of the RMT. Each stage deserves its own book so while I reference these other important aspects of the video production process, this book does not attempt to explore them in any depth.

> **This book is for videographers making short factual videos such as Web video.**

PART ONE
Media Communication Basics

Effective videographers are effective communicators. In Part One we explore the dynamics of communication, how communication happens and what it means for video.

PART ONE

COMMUNICATION AND VIDEO

IT'S NOT "COPY AND PASTE"

Good videographers are good communicators. So before we get into the nitty-gritty of video scripts, let's explore some of the dynamics of communication. In particular, I'd like to question the popular assumption that communicating is simply about crafting the perfect message. If it were, communication would merely be a matter of copying and pasting our message from one brain to another. I wish it was that simple. But communication is much more messy, unpredictable and convoluted.

Folks with a "copy and paste" mindset pour over their message to ensure it is just right. You have probably come across people like this. They fuss over grammar, font sizes on slide decks, colors and spelling. They grumble when people use nouns like "flag" as verbs but prefer abstract nouns to give their writing gravitas. Some throw in Latin phrases or French expression to add finesse.

Now, don't get me wrong, I'm all for good grammar and the artful use of language. And I enjoy French expressions because French is my favorite language. But sometimes we get so bogged down in crafting the message to be sure it is "correct," or impresses our audience, that we actually make our message harder to understand. In video we spend so much time worrying about style or adding fancy effects our message is drowned out.

When it comes to effective communication, the style of our message is less important than whether it has been easily understood by our audience. But that's often the opposite of what is taught so it becomes easy to hide behind excuses such as, "Oh, it had eloquent language," or, "It was grammatically correct," or, "It's a really nice font," rather than facing the fact that sometimes our message simply was not understood. Videographers hide behind, "Nice transition..." or, "We used green screen..." or, "We shot it in 4k...", but more often than not, these have much less effect on how the message is understood than we think.

Communication is not about impressing people with fancy words, devices or literary style. It is about being understood. No understanding = no communication.

> **Effective communicators focus first on how to be understood rather than designing flashy messages**

It's Their Message

Another presumption I would like to challenge as we explore communication is the notion that our message will be completely understood. For example, when I explain how to check in at an airport, I assume my communication partner will have exactly the same picture in her head as I do about the process. But this isn't so. In fact most of the time her vision of checking in, based on my description, will be very, very different.

But today a lot of communication is taught based on this unrealistic assumption. You find books written on how to phrase an answer in a job interview, what words to use in a sales call or how to craft the perfect message. But communication is messy and unpredictable. What you put in your message is almost certainly going to be different to what your communication partner understands. I would suggest that as we communicate we need to strive not for exact understanding – because it's impossible – but for the closest understanding.

Let's explore this by breaking down the way communication happens. We take four steps as we work towards closest understanding.

First, we structure our message. This is where we scrutinize our content and review it. For a presentation it may be writing a script or creating a slide deck. If it's a video it will involve drawing a storyboard and writing a script.

Second, we transmit it. This could be hitting "Send" on your email program or uploading your video to YouTube. At this point, as a communicator, we are letting go of our message. It no longer belongs to us.

Third, our communication partner receives and filters our message. She filters it through her experiences, education and interests. She will ignore some parts of our message but remember other bits. Numerous factors influence which parts of our message she ignores. They could include what interests her, makes sense to her and whether or not she is distracted by something else.

Fourth, she constructs her version of your message. Now the message is hers. Using the parts of your message she did not ignore, she will construct your message in her mind. It is now her message. Often we will have no idea which part of our message she tuned out. But if she tuned out an important part – perhaps she was distracted – then the integrity of our original message was significantly compromised.

It is risky to assume communication is simply a matter of crafting a message that will be easily understood because that's not how things happen. You share information and hope that important parts of what you share will not be ignored. That way, your communication partner will have everything she needs to build an understanding that is closest to what you intended.

Messages hidden behind big words, fancy expressions or techniques motivated by aesthetic values have to work harder to break through. Likewise in video, messages obscured by indulgent special effects or pictures that are irrelevant will create an experience but not necessarily a shared understanding.

The factual videographer's role is to share the pictures, words, music, sound effects and text graphics that have the highest likelihood of being used (rather than ignored). Your viewer can then contruct her own understanding of the message, that is as similar as possible to yours.

If you see your role as being a video artist, your success comes down to how well you create an experience. You might do this by emulating a Stephen Spielberg technique or incorporate a trick you saw in a Clint Eastwood movie. You might copy the editing style of CSI Miami or American Idol. But if you see your role as a *video communicator*, your success will come down to how well you choose and combine these elements so your viewer adopts many of them to create her understanding. Ultimately, your success will depend on how good you are at choosing the right elements for your video that grab her attention, and carry the most meaning, to enable her to create a deeper, richer experience.

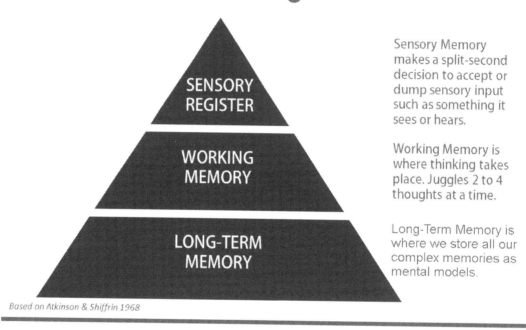

Your Viewer's Brain Wants to Reject Most of What it Sees

Experts say the brain takes in information and processes it using three distinct stages of memory. This is based on a model developed by Atkinson & Shiffrin in the late sixties which is still broadly used by academics today to explain communication.

What we see, hear, feel, taste and smell is really just a memory. After all, what you taste is momentary and what you saw a moment ago is no longer here. The brain processes these memories through the:

- Sensory Register
- Working Memory
- Long-Term Memory

> **Videographers choose pictures, words and other message elements they think are least likely to be dumped or discarded. They use as few elements as possible to prevent sensory bottleneck.**

Sensory Register – Master Dumper

Anything you see or hear, such as a video, enters the Sensory Register which is said to filter out anything it considers irrelevant. Filtering is done in a millisecond. The Sensory Register is also known as the Sensory Memory.

For example, you're watching a news reporter talking live on camera and someone walks behind the journalist. This is a visual memory and your brain quickly decides whether to think about that person (memory) or ignore them. Most likely, your brain will discard that piece of visual memory. However, if that person was your favorite music artist, your Sensory Register will tag that visual memory as important rather than discard it.

The Sensory Register has a very limited capacity, less than a second. So as it takes everything in, it tries to dump as much as it can. If it didn't do this, everything we see and hear would get backed up and cause sensory bottleneck. It's fair to say the Sensory Register is really a "Master Dumper." It has its own ways of determining what to dump but generally it includes sensory information that's boring, non-threatening, unfamiliar and irrelevant.

The Working Memory – Where You Think About Stuff

When the Sensory Register tags a memory as relevant – like the image of your favorite music artist walking behind the reporter – it is passed into the second stage of memory, the Working Memory. This stage of memory is like a thinking space. One way to think of it is as the RAM of your computer. So when a potential client watching your yoga video tries to copy your moves, it is in his Working Memory that he makes sense of it. When someone is moved by your motivational video, it's all happening in his Working Memory.

It's believed people can juggle between two and four thoughts in their brains at any one time. So as someone watches your PR video, he may be thinking about his vacation, what time he has to pick the kids up from childcare and an email he sent that afternoon. Asking him to process more information will create significant pressure on the brain and slows everything down. It's like running several software programs at the same time on a computer with low RAM.

When we communicate, we need to capture our viewers' attention so their other thoughts are not a distraction. We also need to manage the amount of information we share so it doesn't lead to cognitive overload. This is the reason simple is always best when packaging your messages. In video, a lot of this is done visually so it's something we focus on when we do our storyboard.

Your Viewer Builds Understanding Using Long-Term Memories

We just talked about a famous music artist walking behind a reporter on live TV. Fans instantly recognize her thanks to an efficient Sensory Register. But how does the Sensory Register know to tag that image and not dump it?

The answer lies in the Long-Term Memory which is where our older memories are stored. This includes past events, beliefs, values and practical knowledge such as how to tie a shoelace. Fans of this particular artist have memories of her in

> **" Viewers use existing memories to make sense of new information coming through the Sensory Register "**

their Long-Term Memory. The Sensory Register recognizes this so the visual memory is tagged and the Working Memory pulls these memories in from the Long-Term Memory.

The Working Memory pulls on existing memories to make sense of new memories. For example, when I see a stop sign, my memory of the Department of Motor Vehicles rule book, stored in the Long-Term Memory, pops into my Working Memory and I know to hit the brakes.

The brain is an amazing creation. It works efficiently to manage the sensory deluge you face every day, sifting through images, scents, tastes, tactile sensations and sounds to make sure your brain gets the information it needs for survival.

MEDIA COMMUNICATION BASICS

Long-Term Memories are Stored in Mental Models

The Long-Term Memory is said to have an indefinite capacity to hold memories. Each of these memories is a mental model which arranges lots of smaller memories, scattered around the brain, into single patterns that help your brain understand things in context.

Mental models help you navigate and survive in the world. For example, you have a mental model about what an accelerator pedal is. You know that pushing the accelerator will move your car forward. If you find yourself in the driver's seat of a bus, you'll use that memory to understand the bus is likely to move forward if you press the accelerator. We use existing memories to make sense of new situations. We think a lot about mental models when developing the structure and narrative of our videos, which is Step 4 of the Rapid Video Technique.

Here's why all this is important. You might craft the perfect video message based on what makes sense to you. But due to the simple reality that we all view things through different experiences, your message may be interpreted in many different ways. Our challenge is to know our audience, their language, experiences and aspirations as well as we can.

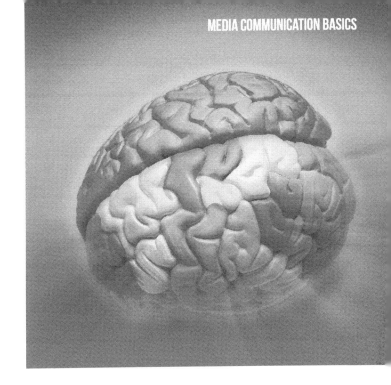

Implications for the Video Script Writer

Understanding how the brain works gives us some key principles for communicating. Here are some important ones:

First, every picture, sequence, voice over, sound effect and piece of music needs to appeal to the Sensory Register. If not, the Sensory Register will dump it. We need to think about this with both word choice and sentence structure.

Second, our message needs to be as light as possible. The Sensory Register has an extraordinarily limited capacity to process everything it sees, hears, smells, touches and tastes. That means fewer words, fewer pictures and fewer flashy effects are best.

Third, we must understand our message through our viewers' experiences, not ours. That's not to say our experiences and instincts are unimportant, but it's easy to forget many people see our messages very differently.

Fourth, we need to keep the cognitive load of our messages low. If someone needs to watch your video twice to understand your message, the cognitive load is probably too heavy. This requires us to strip our message down to it's most basic delivery using as few pictures and words as we can.

Fifth, we need to understand the language, emotions, world views, needs and interests of our audience so we can package our message to make sense to them. Words mean different things to different people. News events evoke different reactions. Pictures may tell a thousand words, but most often, they are different words for different folks. So getting to know our audience is critical.

The Life of a Message

How does all this look in the life of a simple message? Consider I am watching TV...

1. TV shows a wide shot of traffic on a freeway. This is not interesting to me so my Sensory Register dumps it.

2. Camera cuts to a wide shot of the White House in Washington, DC. I follow politics closely so it triggers a collection of memories in my Long-Term Memory about the presidential primaries. So my Sensory Register tags the image.

3. Now the image has been tagged, my Working Memory takes it and thinks about it. It pulls up everything I know about the primaries from my Long-Term Memory. As I sift through these, I remember today is the Iowa Straw Poll.

Modalities, Not Multimedia

In the rapid media technique, we don't refer to audio, video, screen text, animation and games as multimedia because they sit on the new medium which is the Web. We refer to these as modalities rather than media.

4. Next the TV shows a close up of one of the major candidates. My Sensory Register tags her memory which moves to my Working Memory from my Long-Term Memory, and I remember she was in the news for corruption.

5. We then see a journalist talking live on camera. This imagery is boring so my Sensory Register dumps it. But I hear the words, "Three points up."

6. Drawing on my knowledge of vocabulary, I am able to piece together that the story was about a primary candidate's polling improving despite her corruption scandal

My ability to understand this message relied on my Sensory Register letting through the key message elements. If it had dumped, for example, the picture of the White House I would have missed this message.

All sorts of things could derail my message. My mind could be pre-occupied with three or four other topics. I might be distracted visually by something outside the scope of the television set and missed the cues. Or I could have had the wrong associations with different people in the picture.

There's a lot that can go wrong in communication, so understanding its dynamics is critical. When it comes to writing video scripts, we need to be focused on our message objective and ask ourselves, what will be the best media elements to give our viewers so they can clearly and easily construct the message in their minds?

Because the Sensory Register has to make split-second decisions about what pictures, sounds and words to take in we need to use elements that are most likely to be accepted. That means pictures that are most likely to be quickly recognized. Words and sentences that are simple and short and don't take the Sensory Register much time to determine whether they are relevant

Knowing the Working Memory does not have the capacity to work with too many ideas at once, we need to keep our content simple. If you have one message objective rather than two or more, it will be easier for viewers to understand your message.

We also know people interpret your message through their own experiences so tapping into known experiences within your audience will be a benefit too.

The writing techniques we look at in Part Four are based on this understanding of communication. Before we get to that, we need to consider video psychology which we explore in Part Three.

PART ONE

MEDIA COMMUNICATION BASICS

PART ONE – EASY REFERENCE

COMMUNICATION

- Communication is about working towards shared understanding
- Communication is messy, unpredictable and convoluted
- Your communication partner builds and owns your message
- Messages pass through 3 stages of memory:
    - Sensory Register
    - Working Memory
    - Long-Term Memory
- The Sensory Register dumps as much of what it sees and hears as it can to reduce sensory bottleneck. It does this in a split-second
- The Working Memory processes sensory messages drawing on the Long-Term Memory
- People use mental models in the Long-Term Memory to understand your message

VIDEO IMPLICATIONS

- As we create video, we need to:
    - Choose words that appeal to the Sensory Register
    - Keep our messages simple
    - Understand the experiences our audience will use to interpret our message

PART TWO
Video Psychology

Good video is a powerful combination of pictures, music, spoken word and other message layers. In Part Two we explore how they work together to create a powerful video.

PART TWO

HOW VIDEO WORKS

Video is not good for conveying all types of information. It's good when the viewer can see lots of action and visually interesting shots. But if there's no action, viewers will lose interest. And if the message has a complex narrative or needs a lot of detail to be understood, such as facts and figures, it will be tough to use a visual story.

For example, someone walking a dog makes good video. Someone talking about it doesn't. A video showing how to change a tire would make a good video but not someone talking to the camera and explaining it. Pictures are what carry the message in video. There's a saying in the TV news business that summarizes the priority of pictures. "If it bleeds, it leads." A story showing a car wreck will more likely draw a viewer's eye than a politician giving a speech from behind a podium.

Video is About Pictures

When we watch video, our minds are drawn to what we see in the video rather than what we hear spoken. If this surprises you, think back to the last time you watched a weather forecast on television. Can you remember the words the forecaster used? Most people can't. However, most remember what they saw on the screen such as radar maps and graphics. This happens when they watch your video – viewers remember what they see more than the voice over or monologue. For this reason, talking head videos are incredibly ineffective at anything other than letting viewers see what the speaker looks like. And because the audience takes in information for no more than about 10 seconds, anything after that will be lost.

Video is primarily about pictures. So it makes more sense to plan your pictures, which people remember, before thinking about the words, which viewers will most likely forget. However, some people spend the bulk of their time crafting their script and then at the last moment, they go looking for pictures to match their words. This makes no sense. Why invest the bulk of your time writing a nice script that viewers will forget? And then spend so little time on what viewers will remember, the pictures? It also makes little sense to make pictures that are slaves to words rather than words that enhance the pictures.

Just as words are a language, pictures are too. Good video communicators learn the language and grammar of pictures. They study camera angles, shot sizes, composition, camera movements, positions, lighting, and so forth. This is their language. And it's why in the rapid video technique we always start with pictures before writing the script and adding music or sound effects.

Video is a Series of Message Layers

Video works powerfully as a series of different message layers, each of which plays an interdependent role in crafting the message. These are:

- Picture layer
- Visual Effects layer
- Animation layer
- Text Graphics layer
- Graphics layer
- Spoken Word layer
- Music layer
- Sound Effects layer

Each of these layers has its own grammar, or set of rules, to make your message easier to follow. For example, visual grammar is about framing each shot and cutting them together to appear natural while communicating the message.

In this book we are looking primarily at the spoken word layer and how to express it in your video script. Like the picture layer, the spoken word has its own set of rules, or grammar, which are quite different from the written word. This is an important point because people often follow written grammar when writing scripts, which actually makes understanding more difficult.

With the exception of the picture layer, which always has priority, all layers are equal. The picture layer is the foundational layer and carries the story. Pictures are so important in video that Alfred Hitchcock called silent movies the purist form of cinema.

After the pictures have been determined, all the other layers work together to fill in any gaps that may have been left by the picture layer. Not all messages layers need to be used.

Let's consider we have a sequence of pictures of a man walking into a dangerous alley in New York

City. While the pictures make some of the danger apparent, we may want the viewer to know how this man feels as he steps into the unknown. So we turn to other message layers to add this crucial part of the story. We could use the spoken word layer, such as a voice over along the lines of, "This man is walking into danger." But that sounds pretty lame. We could express the danger by overlaying the picture with a caption that says, "Dangerous alley." This is as bad as the voice over because it still takes time for the immediate impact to be felt. However, we can probably find a melodramatic piece of music that instantly evokes a foreboding feel. Weighing up all our options, music will be the best tool to convey our message.

How Should I use Different Message Layers?

The question many people ask is when do we use each different layer? Well it's about balancing the narrative strength of each layer as they work to support the pictures. And while every professional will have a different view, I'll share my thoughts while acknowledging there are many different opinions. So as a starting point, here's what I suggest you consider.

Picture layer

This is your sequence of video shots that carry the bulk of your message. It's good for action and keeping your viewer engaged. The picture layer works well with concrete details like close-ups of gadgets, actions with lots of movement and truly unique visuals.

Visual Effects layer

This is where you manipulate the picture layer for a narrative purpose. Usually this is because the video picture does not make your point clear enough. Or you need to draw the viewer's eye. For example, we might add a sepia tone effect to convey we're going back in time. Or use a fuzzy dissolve to create the illusion of a flashback. There are many visual effects at your disposal in today's modern editing software.

Animation layer

Animation can include good old fashioned cartoons or simulations of things like how a piston works in a car engine. Animation can add a fun feel to your pictures when used as cartoons. It also works well for manipulating objects or characters in unnatural or impossible ways. For example, animated cartoons can exaggerate facial features of politicians. When explaining a technical process, you can slow down the motion, create cutaways and do pull-outs.

Text Graphics layer

Text graphics are text overlaid on the screen. For example, a black screen with simple white words conveying a message. Or text in the lower thirds showing someone's name as they speak on camera. Lists of credits are also part of the text layer. Text graphics are good for reinforcing key details that would be cumbersome to convey in other ways.

Graphics layer

Graphics refer to static images that communicate ideas such as pie charts, icons or logos. Graphics are great for quickly showing relationships which are not immediately clear in the pictures. Rather than describing how congress works, a graphic that shows the two legislative chambers may get the message across in a fraction of the time of spoken word content.

Spoken Word layer

Spoken word is anything that is spoken by a human. It includes voice overs, dialogue and monologues. The spoken word is good for adding details to pictures such as names, ideas, thoughts or information such as the year or piece of data. It is good for dialogue in interviews and role plays so we can hear the person's personality.

Music layer

Music adds mood and energy to your pictures. It also helps draw on the viewer's long-term memories to transport them somewhere else. A great example of this is music from another culture which evokes images of its people and customs.

Sound Effects layer

Sound effects can add gritty realism to your message which draw in an emotional element from memories associated with key sounds in the Long-Term Memory.

Seamless Integration

Message layers should integrate seamlessly as the videographer uses whichever most efficiently conveys the message. A good videographer is always subtle when weaving this tapestry together because exaggerated use of effects or music can draw attention to the technique, and we don't want that. We want it drawn to the message.

PART TWO

PART TWO - EASY REFERENCE

VIDEO AS A COMMUNICATION MODALITY

- Video works as a series of message layers to convey the message
- Message layers include pictures (video footage), visual effects, animation, text graphics, spoken word, music and sound effects
- Pictures are the leading message layer and carry most of the story because people mostly watch rather than listen to video
- Experienced videographers weave the message layers into a rich tapestry that tells a story and engages the viewer
- Video is excellent for conveying action and compelling visuals but struggles to efficiently communicate details and complexity

PART THREE
Video Scripts

Writing for the ear requires us to adopt a different mindset than we have when writing the printed word. In Part Three we explore key principles of this mindset.

WHY WRITE A SCRIPT?

Parts 1 and 2 were all about the dynamics of communication. We had to explore communication before digging into the "nitty gritty" of media writing. Many of us were schooled in the traditional approach to communication which doesn't prepare us very well for the demanding needs of media messaging. (The traditional approach also fails to prepare us for effective communication in the workplace and everyday life, but that's another story). The techniques we are about to discuss are best understood in light of what we've discussed so far.

For some people it can seem easier not to write a script. They've done OK before and are happy to wing it so they grab their camera and start shooting. Sometimes their videos are great, but more often, they are just acceptable. You see a lot of these on YouTube in the way of product demonstrations, promos for small businesses and even "How To" videos on Tai Chi.

People choose to "wing it" rather than "plan it" for many reasons. Some folks ask, if they can re-take bungled footage or fix it in post, why waste time writing it all up in advance? Others have told me they're good talkers, so a script is superfluous. Others admit they're just plain lazy. I feel these are all flawed arguments.

There are compelling reasons for writing a script. The best is it saves you time. This may sound counter-intuitive if you just want to get out and shoot video, but a good script prevents problems that will need extra time to fix. Fixing problems usually takes twice as long as getting things right the first time.

Here are just a few reasons to script your videos.

1. **Scripts keep your team on the same page**
   If you have more than one person working on a project, having a script means everyone is on the same page. If three people are doing things differently and making the video up as they go along, they'll be working to different assumptions. This becomes a huge problem when you get together and edit your material.

2. **Scripts ensure consistency for editing**
   If you are adlibbing and need four takes, it's almost impossible to say the same thing exactly the same way during each take. In the first take you emphasize one word. In the next take you emphasize another word. In the third, you use a different word or intonation that doesn't match the other takes. How do you edit all that? It rarely flows nicely so you end up wasting more time in post production trying to make these four different takes work together as one.

3. **Takes get worse every time you do another**
   Here's an interesting experience a lot of people discover the hard way when they have to take a shot more than once or twice. Usually the first two takes are best. As you get down to your fourth and fifth take, your performance starts to get worse. Don't believe me? Try it.

4. **Scripts enable you to sound and look better**
   One of the problems of adlibbing without a script is your brain allocates half its resources to work out what words to use and how to put them in order. This leaves only half of your resources to focus on the presentation. When you have a script to follow, your brain can give most of its resources to sounding good because it doesn't have to spend important presentational energy finding words. This frees you up to think about breathing, intonation, diction and so forth.

5. **Scripts ensure brand or message consistency**
   This is big in corporate video, especially where you have branding issues and want to be sure everything looks and sounds consistent. A script keeps you from forgetting the important stuff so you don't have to go back and shoot it all again.

6. **Well-written scripts are easier to understand**
   If you're writing for video, you need to think carefully about every word and how it relates to each picture. Writing a script gives you the time to put all the techniques into place that we're about to talk about. If you don't write a script, you'll be spending a split second on every word. Is that enough to choose the right words and put them in an order that will be quick and easy to understand?

SPOKEN WORD IN VIDEO

There's every chance I'm preaching to the choir—you bought this book because you want to make your videos quicker and easier to understand. However, in case you're reading this because your boss told you to, let me share one of the first principles I learned in my early broadcast training. I was told, "The best adlibs are scripted." In more than twenty-five years of media work I have personally found scripts save you loads of time and almost always ensure a better product.

The video script is primarily about the spoken word message layer. Yes, it will most likely describe what the viewer sees and when you are likely to drop some music in the background. But we primarily use it to plan what is heard by the viewer. As a script writer, you'll most likely be writing one of the following forms of spoken word content:

- Commentary
- Monologue
- Dialogue

Commentary is spoken word content where the viewer does not see the person speaking. Also known as a voice over, it is common in documentaries and advertisements. Commentary is totally subservient to the picture, which we'll discuss in more detail in a few moments.

A monologue features the speaker on camera talking directly to the viewer. Generally one person is involved in a monologue, but it can also include two people like on network news broadcasts when the people on screen reference each other while really talking to the viewer. The best example of a monologue is the classic talking head shot. Another example is a reporter reporting from a live event.

Dialogue is spoken word content that takes place between multiple people on screen. We see dialogue in television drama where it's part of the writer's strategy to develop character and plot. Character and plot are beyond the scope of this book – our focus is on short web videos you might use to advertise your business or convey an important message within your organization.

The primary focus of this book is commentary (voice overs).

PRINCIPLES OF WRITING VIDEO SCRIPTS

It's easy to think writing a video script is simply about tapping away on your keyboard to get your message across. As we discussed earlier, communication is much more complex. What your viewer understands depends on the memories in your viewer's Long-Term Memory and how well you choose sensory stimuli to trigger the most appropriate memories.

When it comes to video, there are further complexities to add. Here are some important principles to communicate your message well in the video modality.

1. Your message must be quick and easy to understand.
2. Your spoken word content needs to be written with every message layer in mind..
3. The words you choose should support (not repeat) the picture layer.
4. Your words and sentences need to have an aural quality.
5. Your message will be quicker and easier to understand if written in a conversational tone.

Spoken Word: Quick and Easy to Understand

The universal rule for any media communication is that your message must be quick and easy to understand. If your viewer is left scratching his head wondering what your message was, you failed. If he has to watch it again to make sense of it, you failed. The writing techniques in this book are all designed to make your spoken word content easier to understand.

We need to choose words and structure our sentences so they are less likely to be discarded when they hit the Sensory Register. We need to reduce cognitive load so the Working Memory is not overwhelmed. And we need to choose words, stories and metaphors familiar to our viewer and likely to be in his Long-Term Memory.

Our ultimate goal is to share as much information using the fewest media elements. That is, the

PART THREE

fewest words, pictures, music, sound effects and so forth. Incidentally, the clearer your editorial purpose, the easier this process is. A clear purpose can act as a yardstick to help you decide which media elements are unnecessary.

Write with Every Message Layer in Mind

A lot of organizations ask people in their teams who are good at writing reports and editing other people's work to write their video scripts. Often these folks write user manuals or do instructional design and are known to have a friendly streak of "grammar righteousness."

When you read their video scripts you find they have followed every rule of grammar. Actually, these scripts are a delight to read. But they're not a delight to listen to while watching video. The rules of written grammar are the wrong rules to follow. Written grammar evolved to make it easier to read. However, your script is not being read by your viewer. It is being listened to as your listener also watches the pictures.

So what's the difference? When people read, the message is completely captured by the words. They do the heavy lifting in terms of communication. In video, words work with other message layers to convey the complete meaning.

Poor Voice Over
"Roger and Kim were looking at the internet"

Better Voice Over
Kim and Roger will nominate the best photo from the office party.

Part of the message will be in the picture while part will be in the emotion and the other may be in the spoken word.

Support the Picture Layer

A constant theme in this book is that pictures are the most important part of video. This is because people focus more on what they see than what they hear. Words, therefore, must defer to the picture. To reduce cognitive load, we should only use words when pictures don't stand on their own. Use words to fill a gap. Use words to explain something important to your message that may not be clear in the picture. But don't repeat in your commentary what is obvious in the picture.

For example, consider you have a wide shot of a boat speeding down a river. The voice over, "This boat is speeding down the river," adds nothing to the message. It just adds another sensory element for your Sensory Register to process. It possibly increases sensory bottleneck. And if it tags the commentary for the Working Memory, it asks the Working Memory to do the same thing it did with the visual. This duplication increases the cognitive load. However, "Tom Smith's new engine reduces emissions," would work. We can see from the picture it's a boat, but we can't see it's Tom Smith's engine or the significance.

Write Aurally

Words in video are heard: with the exception of titles and text graphics. So it's important to consider their phonetic quality. This is important at two levels. First, the word choice itself. And second, the way words go together.

Words with crisp, clear consonants like "d" "k" or "t" are easier to recognize than words with soft consonants like "c" "g" "h" or "l".

Some consonant sounds are more difficult for the ear to distinguish than others. For example, "m" and "n" can be confused when spoken quickly as can, "b" and "p." Listen to words carefully to be sure they are easy to recognize.

When we speak, we often run words together. On paper, the eye can see where one word starts and ends. But the ear can't. For example, read this phrase out loud: "Increasing attacks on senior citizens." The word, "attacks," sounds like "a tax." It is fine on paper but not good on the ear.

So when you write, think about how the words sound and review everything by reading it out loud. If you can, read your script out loud to someone else for feedback.

Also: consider the person who will read your script. We all sound different and one phrase may work better for one person than another.

PART THREE

Write Conversationally

Communication going back to the beginning of time was always a conversation. It's just that as oral storytelling was replaced by cave paintings, which were replaced by printed books and then later radio and television, we lost the immediate feedback loop. But viewers still feel a certain relationship going on between them and the content.

Write as if you are in a conversational relationship with the viewer. Formality makes things more difficult to understand usually involving big words that a lot of people don't recognize and formal sentence structures that generally contain too many words. Writing in an informal tone keeps the cognitive load low and avoids sensory bottleneck as there is less work for your brain.

Another important consideration when adopting a conversational tone is to write as if you are speaking to only one person. This will make it feel more personal. The instant you use phrases like, "My audience," or "People out there," you make your viewer feel as if they are one of a crowd. When you skip, "My audience will find," and instead say, "You will find," it feels much more personal. The more personal you are the more engaging your content.

SCRIPT LAYOUT

It really doesn't matter how you lay out your video script. The important thing is to make it clear so you and your team can read it easily.

If you're writing a TV drama or a screenplay for Hollywood, it's a different matter. You are expected to follow a set of conventions that are quite rigid. They involve a specific typeface, defined margins, line spacing and the need for each page to last for a minute of screen time.

Fortunately, we're not working in Hollywood. Follow a visual format that makes sense for you. I know journalists who write their scripts on scraps of paper and I have corporate clients who incorporate their storyboards into their scripts. Really, it's about what makes it easier for you and your team to shoot terrific video and stay on the same page.

For what it's worth, I follow a three column formula. If you're just exploring how to lay out your scripts you could try this and adapt it to your work. I have taken the classic documentary script which features two columns and added a third column. In the left hand column of the classic documentary script, the writer describes what viewers will see. This could be, "Warehouse: Wide Shot of Freda Bloomsbury lifting boxes in Aisle 47. Freda places box on mid-shelf then turns to camera and speaks." The right hand column is used to describe what viewers will hear which includes spoken word, music and sound effects. It could be, "Background atmosphere. Freda: It's easy to get hurt lifting boxes in the warehouse."

A three column format, which you can see on this page, adds a third column to the left side of the page. In it, I recommend you write the number of each shot. When you're doing short videos this may seem tedious, but it's a great habit to adopt. When you are doing a lot of production, it will make your work easier to manage. You may find yourself shooting multiple scenes out of order or even shooting several different videos at once. While we are not talking about production management, this column is one piece of information you will need to develop a shot plan.

WORKPLACE SAFETY VIDEO

Writer: Tanya Smith
Phone: X 6764
Date: 7/28/14

1	EXTERNAL: Extra Wide Shot of Warehouse entrance	Short music piece. Fades as we cut to shot 3
2	INTERNAL: Wide shot of Freda Bloomsbury lifting boxes onto Shelf in Aisle 47	
3	INTERNAL: Mid shot of Freda as she places box on middle shelf then turns to camera	**Freda:** It's easy to get hurt.
4	INTERNAL: Wide shot of Forklift moving boxes into Aisle 47	**Freda:** That's why we're serious about safety everywhere in the warehouse
5	INTERNAL: Mid shot of Freda standing in front of shelf, talking to camera	**Freda:** Something as simple as lifting a box can do it

PART THREE

PART THREE – EASY REFERENCE
VIDEO SCRIPTS

- Save time and money
- Ensure message impact
- Should be quick and easy to understand
- Use spoken word content as a support to the picture
- Need to consider the aural quality of words and sentences
- Can have three columns: one for shot number, another for shot description and another for spoken word and music

PART FOUR

The Practice of Writing a Video Script

The words you choose and the way you put them together can profoundly affect your video's impact. In Part Four we look at specific writing techniques to make your video quick and easy to understand.

PART FOUR

WRITING YOUR SCRIPT

We've discussed generally how communication works best, applied it to video and explored what video does well as a medium. We've also talked about the role spoken word has in video messages. Now it's time to take these principles and put them into action. Here are four areas we're going to explore:

1. Picture-word relationship
2. Tone
3. Sentence construction
4. Word choice

When you write your video script, your primary purpose is to create shared understanding. We know communication is messy and it will never be perfect so we work to improve our chances of being understood by following a number of strategies. These include using recognizable media elements, avoiding sensory bottleneck and reducing cognitive load.

Using recognizable media elements means choosing pictures, words, metaphors and other media elements that are easy for viewers to recognize. They can then use experiences in their Long-Term Memories to understand our message. Avoiding sensory bottleneck involves choosing words our Sensory Register can quickly identify as either relevant or irrelevant and keeping our sentences short. So this is about word choice and understanding our viewer's likely experiences.

Reducing cognitive load means being disciplined to include just one editorial purpose per video and ruthlessly reviewing every element of our videos to ensure everything is aligned with the one purpose. If you follow these three strategies, you will improve your chances of achieving shared understanding.

Disciplined writers are motivated by the understanding aspect of communication. They don't spend time looking for fancy words, they look for effective words. They don't cram voice overs into every moment of silence, they allow pictures to breathe and speak on their own. (Only when the picture is not easy to understand do they add the words.)

In a sense, professional video script writers are frugal writers. They see every word as worth ten dollars so they use them sparingly. They only use words when they have to. Amateur writers, however, write with flourish and spend words as if they're worth nothing.

So how do we achieve this economic approach to writing? We start with a clearly defined purpose for every visual sequence. At first, this feels cumbersome but after some time, you'll find it is second nature and a healthy habit.

How does this process look in reality? Let's say I need to convey "Stephen is late for a 3pm appointment with his doctor in Manhattan. Stephen is always late for his appointments and, as usual, he ends up having to take a taxi instead of walking."

My first task is to think about what shots I can use to express this. After I have worked this out I need to consider the shots in sequence and evaluate if my message is clear. Take a look at the storyboard on the next page.

PART FOUR

Extreme Wide shot:
New York skyline.

Wide shot:
Stephen walks purposefully along 7th Avenue. Then he looks across the road (where taxis drive by).

Close up:
Taxi sign on top of car.

Mid shot:
Stephen looks at his watch. Facial expression of worry.

Mid shot:
Doctor reviewing his calendar.

Close up:
Doctor's calendar shows Stephen's name at 3pm.

Over the Shoulder:
Stephen's watch showing 2:55pm.

Wide shot:
Taxi driving down 7th Avenue.

Mid wide shot:
Stephen on side of road hails cab.

The first shot (the establishment shot) is clear we are in Manhattan, New York. It's an iconic shot familiar to most people.

The second shot of Stephen on 7th Avenue clearly identifies it is a man, but not that it is Stephen. Do we need to identify him? Well it depends on the bigger story of which this sequence is a part. Let's say the viewer already knows it is Stephen. Given this, we don't need to do anything about identifying him such as imposing a caption (or lower third), on the screen with his name.

The third shot shows a taxi cab driving by. It's a close-up of the taxi sign on top of the roof. We know the taxi is significant because Stephen looked in that direction at the end of the previous shot.

The fourth shot is of him looking at his watch. His face is wrinkled with concern. We don't know what the time is, but it is obviously of concern to him.

To explain that Stephen needs to be at his doctor's office, we cut to a mid shot of his doctor behind a desk reviewing a document that looks like his schedule. We know this man is a doctor because he's wearing a stethoscope. We then cut to a close-up of the schedule and it shows the 3:00pm slot of his calendar with Stephen's name clearly written in.

Now we cut back to a close up of Stephen's watch

Now we cut back to a close up of Stephen's watch which reads 2:55 pm. Now we know he's late because we just saw the schedule with his name.

Next we cut to the shot of the taxi driving down 7th Avenue and finally a mid shot of Stephen hailing the taxi.

The key to writing a video script is allowing the picture all the space it needs to convey the message. As we review the sequence of shots, we see they clearly tell us a lot of what is going on. However, they neither tell us Stephen is usually late nor does it convey as much as we want of his sense of panic. So we need to use other message layers for this and the spoken word is the obvious choice.

So how do we do this? In this case all we need is a simple voice such as, "Yet again."

Writing the Script

1. Always start with the pictures
2. Allow the pictures to breathe
3. Use words when the shots are unable to tell the full story

PART FOUR

If we followed written grammar conventions, our voice over would be, "Yet again Stephen left late and ended up having to catch a cab to see his doctor." But none of this is necessary because the pictures speak for themselves.

As we have already discussed, a good video scriptwriter tries to say as little as possible. When she can get away with it, she won't have any spoken word content at all. Letting go of words can seem counterintuitive in a society where we are taught about the power of words and how important they are for communication. But video is simply not about words – it is about pictures.

SENTENCES

In traditional grammar, every sentence should have a subject and a predicate. The subject is the person or object of the sentence. And the predicate expresses what is said about the subject or what it does. For example, Cynthia is chewing bubble gum. "Cynthia" is the subject and "chewing bubble gum" is the predicate.

As you know, video writing is different to written grammar because our subject and predicate do not have to be contained in words – they can be disbursed across pictures, spoken word, music and all the other message layers.

So when it comes to Cynthia chewing gum, we might express her chewing gum (the predicate) by showing a close-up of her grinding her jaw or even blowing a bubble. And we might feature the voice over, "Cynthia." Of course the picture will tell us a lot about who Cynthia is too, by the clothes she wears and her facial expression. So unlike written grammar where the sentence and predicate are expressed only in the words, we spread them across different messages layers.

When you start writing video scripts, you may feel uneasy ignoring the rules of written grammar. You might find yourself using just one word when you would have used eight if writing to be read. Don't get turned off by this. By just about every measure, writing for the ear (whether this be for video or audio) almost always looks bland on paper. But it almost always sounds better to the ear.

Rules for Video Sentences

Here are some rules to ensure your sentences make your video easier to understand:

1. Use as few words as possible
2. Avoid tautologies

THE PRACTICE OF WRITING A VIDEO SCRIPT

3. Use simple sentences (in other words, one clause per sentence)

4. Write in the active voice

5. Make sure sentences sound easy to understand

Use as Few Words as Possible

Canadian writing teacher Crawford Killian wrote a killer phrase I've been quoting to my media students for a decade. "Every word must fight for its life." I can't think of a better way to capture the importance of brevity.

When I write a sentence, I usually end up packing it with words I don't need. I then go back and strip them out. When I say words I don't need, I don't mean they're useless. It's that they pad the sentence out or add fluff to it. If I kept these words in my sentences, they would increase the sensory bottleneck because the sentence with more words than it needs gives the Sensory Register more work to do.

If you're like me, and write sentences which need to be cut back, ruthlessly review every sentence and remove words you don't need. How do you know if you don't need it? Ask yourself this simple question, "If I delete this word, does it change my message?"

If your message is still clear when you take that word out, delete it. It's as simple as that. Even if it feels uncomfortable because you now have a sentence with only a subject and no predicate, the predicate is expressed pictorially, so delete it. We're not writing poetry, we're communicating.

Media writers, whether they write for radio or television, break a lot of rules when it makes their content quicker and easier to understand. For example, when you listen to the radio, you don't hear the announcer say, "We're expecting a top temperature of 84 degrees Fahrenheit today." We can take a lot of words out of that sentence and still understand the message. The announcer is more likely to say, "Top of 84." Despite this sentence having no elegance it is much more effective at creating shared understanding because we have reduced sensory bottleneck.

PART FOUR

So how can we keep our sentences economical?

Cut Out Redundant Words

Look at your sentence and remove anything that repeats another word or repeats something that is already expressed by another message layer.

Don't Say:	Instead say:
You will find that next time you log into your computer, you'll be asked to change your password. **18 words**	You'll be asked to change your password next time you log on. **12 words** **Even Better:** You need to change your password next time you log in. **11 words**

Avoid Tautologies

These are words that repeat the meaning of another word. For example, "Welcome Reception" is basically two words that mean the same thing. Have you ever heard of someone holding an "Unwelcome Reception?" A reception is where you welcome people. So using just the word "Reception" is easier to grasp.

I understand there may occasionally be a nuance you want to capture but more often than not, the extra word is clogging up the Sensory Register.

Don't Say:	Instead say:
Attending the new orientation is a basic requirement. **8 words**	Attending orientation is required. **4 words** **Even Better:** You must attend orientation. This is more wordy but it reframes the sentence in the active voice which we discuss below. **4 Words**
The evening sunset was beautiful. He over-exaggerated.	The sunset was beautiful. (Sunset doesn't happen in the morning.) He exaggerated.

THE PRACTICE OF WRITING A VIDEO SCRIPT

Don't Say:	Instead say:
The Arizona ghost town was full of dilapidated ruins.	It was an Arizona ghost town. (What more can I say? First of all, "dilapidated ruins?" That's a tautology. And second, aren't all ghost towns full of ruins?)

Avoid Conjunctions

Avoid conjunctions (which are joining words) such as "and," "but," "so" and "yet." Often you can drop these and simply start a new sentence.

Don't Say:	Instead say:
Yoga can help you in many ways such as providing improvement in your posture and giving you an opportunity to find a state of relaxation. **25 words**	Yoga helps in many ways. It improves posture. And helps you relax. **12 words**

Minimize Adjectives

Adjectives pad out sentences leading to cognitive bottleneck. For example, "Exceedingly hot" is the same as "sweltering" but requires two words. "Sweltering" is also stronger and more descriptive.

If an adjective is so important you simply can't live without it, consider communicating it visually. A close up of someone's face dripping with perspiration beats the word sweltering..

Don't Say:	Instead say:
Peter drives a bright red Ferrari. **6 words**	Peter Drives a Ferrari. **4 words** **You don't need to tell viewers he drives a bright red Ferrari because they should see it is red in the video.**

Use Contractions

Contractions are abbreviations of two words. For example, the contraction of "We will" is, "We'll." Contractions are very common in conversational English but not so much in written English.

(Although, I use them a lot - probably an influence from my broadcasting background.) Contractions help us get our message across faster because we have turned two words into one, reducing the risk of sensory bottleneck. One word of caution, avoid using contractions with international audiences.

Don't Say:	Instead say:
We will	We'll
Do not	Don't
Should not	Shouldn't
She is	She's

Use Simple Sentences

Simple sentences reduce sensory bottleneck and cognitive load. There are three main types of sentence structure. They are:

- Simple
- Compound
- Complex

A simple sentence is almost like a bullet point and has just one clause. A clause is the smallest unit of meaning in a sentence. A clause has a subject and predicate. In other words, an actor and an action.

For example, "John drove his car to the office." Or, "I like watching videos."

A compound sentence has more than one clause. Such as, "John drove to work on a sunny Monday morning." In compound sentences, the two clauses are independent. You could make them two separate sentences and they'll stand on their own. For example, "John drove to work. It was a sunny Monday morning."

A complex sentence has an independent clause PLUS a dependent clause. For example, "John drove to work following his normal route. The first clause, "John drove to work," is independent because it stands on its own. However, "...following his normal route" makes no sense on its own. So it is dependent on the first clause.

Very often, complex sentences will feature the dependent clause interrupting the independent clause. For example, "John drove his car to the office, following his normal route, on a sunny Monday morning." The independent clauses are, "John drove to the office," and, "On a sunny Monday morning." However they are interrupted by the dependent clause, "Following his normal route."

If you write for print, complex sentences are terrific. They add life and finesse. However, when we use complex sentences in spoken word media such as audio or video, they create sensory bottleneck.

When complex sentences hit the Sensory Register, your viewer's brain has to park part of the sentence while it listens to the dependent clause, then pull the first part of the dependent clause: it pulls the first part of the dependent clause back to assemble it with the dependent clause and last part of the independent clause.

It's a three-stage process that just slows everything down. As you'll remember from Part 1, communication isn't something we copy from our brain and paste into the viewer's brain. They take what we share with them (or some of it), and then they do the construction. So when we write complex sentences, we actually make their work harder.

So how do we handle complex sentences? Break them into two separate independent sentences.

I'm sorry to have to dig so deep into grammar and sentence structure, but it really is important. If you load your sentences with more than one clause you're going to create sensory bottleneck, and this makes it harder for the viewer.

I have seen a lot of my students at the university as well as participants in my corporate workshops struggle with this concept. If you find it tough to get your mind around this, don't worry. Just think about writing every sentence as if you are writing a succinct bullet point for a PowerPoint slide. In many ways good video scripts are a series of bullet points each existing to work with other message layers to support your pictures.

Don't Say:	Instead say:
Peter drives a Ferrari, which his wife bought him for Christmas, to the office every day.	Peter drives a Ferrari every day to the office. His wife gave it to him for Christmas.
After John carefully reviewed the division's business plan, he knew his future was assured.	John reviewed the division's business plan carefully. He then knew his future was assured.

Write in the Active Voice

When grammar folks talk about "voice" in a sentence, they are talking about whether the actor or action comes first. When sentences are written in the "active voice" the actor always comes before the action. For example, "Glenda tied her shoelace." Glenda is the actor, and tied is the action. If we wrote this sentence in the passive voice, the action would come first and it would read, "The shoelace was tied by Glenda."

As you can see, sentences written in the active voice tend to be shorter than those in the passive.

voice. In my example above, the active voice has four words and the passive had six. The active voice sentence was shorter by a third. As well as keeping your sentences nice and short, reducing the risk of sensory bottleneck, active voice sentences are more interesting. That's because the first part of it is about the person and we generally like to hear about the person before the action – that's human nature.

Don't Say:	Instead say:
Keeping your entry up to date in the global address book is your responsibility.	You are responsible for keeping your entry current in the global address book. *NOTE: Ordinarily I would have contracted the words "you are." However, when we read the sentence out loud, it sounds like we are saying "your" twice. Not a big deal but making these two similar words sound different helps the Sensory Register differentiate them.*

Don't Say:	Instead say:
The goal of finding strategies to deliver savings to Acme Company's bottom line has been delegated to Abe Smith.	Abe Smith has been given the goal to find savings to Acme Company's bottom line.

Make Sure Sentences Sound Easy to Understand

One of the primary reasons we have to write differently for video (and audio) is we're writing for the ear, not the eye.

When the audience reads the words on paper, they can re-read it and identify each word clearly. When the audience hears the words, many things can prevent them from hearing clearly. This can include the accent of the person reading your script or background noise which can distract your audience or muffle some of your words.

Listening to words via our ears is very different to reading them with our eyes. Years ago I was listening to a fascinating interview on the radio about a guy who wore a mouse suit to school. To be frank, none of it made much sense to me because I'm thinking, "Why would any kid wear a mouse suit to school?" But after a minute or two it became apparent he was talking about a Mao suit.

On paper, Mao suit looks exactly what it is. A Chinese suit designed in the style of Chinese revolutionary leader Mao Tse-tung. When you say Mao suit out loud, the words run together, especially when you say it fast and it sounds to the ear like mouse suit.

How do you avoid these mistakes? Get into the habit of reviewing your scripts out loud. Remember different people can make word combinations sound different. So have your voice over artist read them out and be prepared to make changes once you have heard it.

Don't Say:	Instead say:
... concern about attacks on senior citizens	... concern about violence against senior citizens
... wearing a Mao suit ...	... wearing a Chinese Mao suit ...

WORDS

We've talked about constructing sentences, now we consider the words we use. As I've implied throughout this short book, we're not talking about creative writing such as poetry or literature. Our purpose is shared understanding.

Words and sentences have the practical role of helping create that shared understanding. We don't use them to show off our vocabulary or intimidate people with obscure words. We're not trying to be a modern-day Shakespeare. Words are building blocks.

When I'm asked for feedback on scripts, I usually spend a lot of time asking people why they chose a particular word. I'm not sure why people choose big words. Sometimes I think they're stuck in 2nd Grade when Mrs. Smith offered two gold stars if they put big words in their creative writing projects. Nothing against Mrs. Smith because back then she was trying to expand their vocabulary. But now, they should have an effective vocabulary, and instead of learning new words, they should be using them for the common good.

If they're not stuck in Mrs. Smith's classroom, they're chained to Professor Jones' tutorial room. Too many people in the business world try to impress each other with corporate buzzwords they learned in their MBA studies or heard at a conference. These words don't impress people, they bore them. And they obscure good concrete information. In government, the use of impenetrable language can be a method to crush message clarity. Buzzwords, acronyms and awkward words are generally not helpful when we want to create shared understanding.

When we choose words for our video scripts, our job is to find the one that most clearly gets the message across in the least amount of time. Here are some important principles:

- Link your words to the picture
- Choose simple words
- Lean towards concrete and specific words
- Choose monosyllables over multisyllabic words
- Choose verbs over nouns
- Avoid adverbs

Link Words to Pictures

The picture's role is to lead the narrative, the word's job is to support it. If a picture is unable to convey part of your message, you might consider words. Choose words that specifically follow the theme in the picture.

For example, look at this picture of a traffic jam in Washington, DC on a Friday before a long weekend. We could be neutral and write "Blocked lanes,"

THE PRACTICE OF WRITING A VIDEO SCRIPT

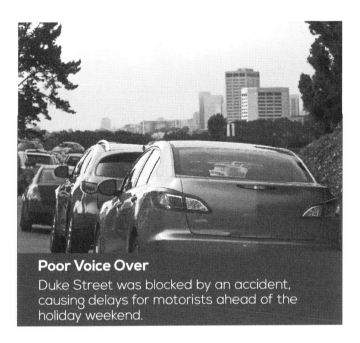

Poor Voice Over
Duke Street was blocked by an accident, causing delays for motorists ahead of the holiday weekend.

Better Voice Over
A car wreck put the brakes on for Duke Street commuters heading home for the holiday weekend.

or "Accident." However, an accident is a broad term that could include a car wreck, spilling a cup of coffee or falling off your bike. So it would be stronger if you used more concrete words such as, "Car wreck." "Blocked" is also a word that can mean many things. Given the picture is about driving home on a holiday weekend, we might even consider, "Putting the brakes on holiday traffic..."

Choose Simple Words

Simple words are usually more familiar to the viewer, take less time to recognize, are easier for the brain to retrieve their meaning from the Long-Term Memory and, more often than not, are short. What is there not to love about simple words?

It can be easy, when we write, to find ourselves in a rut, trapped in a creative cocoon where jargon comes bubbling up in our mind more quickly than words that immediately make sense to our viewer. At other times, when we're not as sure of our meaning as we'd like, larger more ambiguous words give us a little cover.

Ruthlessly review your script to make sure every word is simple and easy to understand. It needs to make immediate sense to the viewer. When I talk about simple, I don't mean simplistic. We're not dumbing down by saying "confused," instead of "discombobulated." We're simply respecting our viewer's time and packaging words so she can use them more easily.

Page 63

If you find yourself coming against a technical term or more complex word that isn't immediately understandable, break it into several words that do make sense for your viewer.

Don't Say:	Instead say:
Transmogrify	Change in a creative way
Beauteous	Beautiful
Tendentious	Biased
Au courant	Well-informed
Surfeit	Excess
Leverage	Take advantage of

Lean towards Concrete and Specific Words

Concrete words represent things you can see, hear, touch, taste or smell. Concrete words make it easier for your viewer to understand your message and includes words such as desk, chair, chocolate or river. When we use them, viewers are very clear about what you mean.

The opposite of concrete words are abstract words, and these are words defining concepts that you can't touch, taste, smell, hear or see. "Freedom" is often used as an example of an abstract word. Unlike a desk, you can't see it. Unlike chocolate you can't taste it.

Remember, meaning is stored in the Long-Term Memory and is both created and refined as it is processed in the Working Memory. To understand what you mean requires a lot more work and some imagination. And almost always, because of the messy nature of communication, abstract words leave much more room for misinterpretation.

You'll notice I haven't urged you to never use abstract words. I'm suggesting you lean towards using concrete words most of the time. But there are instances when abstract words will be just what you need. Aspirational advertising or political campaigns are often well-served by abstract words. Two terrific examples come from campaigns of two presidents who stood for very different ideas.

The first was President Reagan's 1984 campaign ad which started, "It's morning in America." What does that really mean? Morning and sunrise are mostly associated with positive ideas such as a new start. However, the viewer is left to read it through her own positive experiences. Likewise, President Obama's campaign slogan, "Hope and Change" also carries with it positive overtones. What "hope" looks like is actually different for everyone so people would draw their hopes and aspirations from their long-term memories.

Type of Word	What it is	When to Use
Concrete Words	Words that describe what you see, hear, touch, smell and taste. Essential for building up abstract concepts.	Most factual communication that requires people to quickly and easily understand your message.
Abstract Words	Words that don't describe something that hits the senses. Usually it is a concept that takes time to understand.	Aspirational messages where you're happy for different people to read their individual interests into your message.
Onomatopoeia	A word that sounds like the object or action it is describing. For example, "Meow" or "bump."	Regularly throughout your script. Don't overdo it though.
Demonstrative	A word that points to a person or object or infers a person or object. Such as, "Pick that box up," or "Pick that up."	Avoid using demonstratives. They increase word count when pointing to an object or person and are vague when used to infer a person or object.

So abstract language may be appropriate on occasion. But unless it's a very powerful abstract word, it will take your viewer longer to piece together your message. So as I say, lean towards concrete words.

How do we do lean towards concrete words if we have an abstract concept to convey? Explain the abstract concept with concrete words. Let's consider I want viewers to see that retirement from my job offers "freedom." The viewer has to work hard to figure out what freedom means and looks like. However, I can describe freedom with concrete examples. For example, I might say, "Never be tied to your alarm clock. Never report to a boss. And never again worry about those sales figures." Such words bring it alive.

If I am expressing something exciting about a vacation, it would be more invigorating to describe the crunch of sand under my feet or the gentle waves as I throw my line out to catch some fish. As you lean towards using concrete words, remember to keep them simple.

Another technique to help your words become more concrete is to add onomatopoeia. Onomatopoeia refers to words that sound similar to their meaning. For example a whooshing sound actually sounds like the word, "Whoosh." A lot of words have an onomatopoeic quality like "Beep," "Meow," "Bump," "Buzz," "Whoosh," "Click," "Crunch," "Pop," "Revved," "Slash" and there are many more.

While we're talking about concrete words, minimize demonstratives and expletives. Demonstratives are words like "that," "these" and "those." Very often demonstratives are used with other nouns such as, "These cars are hip," or "Those foods are good for an upset tummy." Demonstratives can also be used without the noun and infer the meaning. For example, "These are hip," and "Those are good for an upset tummy."

When you write your video script, unless it is really clear in your picture, try to avoid demonstratives. Use the actual nouns instead. For examples, "Hybrids (cars) are hip," or "Highly acidic foods upset the tummy."

Expletives are indefinite pronouns, and there are two of these in English. "It" and "there." Very often we use expletives instead of nouns. For example, "It stopped working." What wasn't working? A computer? A car? Unless you have the answer clearly in the picture, use a descriptive noun rather than "it." Such as, "The iPad stopped working." Or, "Learning is good for students," rather than, "It is good for them." This principle is even more important in web writing and radio writing because you don't have pictures to carry the message.

Don't Say:	Instead say:
Try not to eat <u>them</u> very often.	Try not to eat <u>fatty foods</u> very often.
I don't appreciate <u>that.</u>	I don't appreciate your <u>comment.</u>
<u>It's</u> a great way to relax.	<u>Yoga</u> is a great way to relax.
If <u>there</u> isn't enough support for the motion.	If enough delegates don't support the motion.

Choose Monosyllable over Multisyllabic Words

I'm a big fan of monosyllables even though some people think they're a tool to "dumb down" the population. Monosyllables are much quicker and easier to process than multisyllables.

A syllable is a basic pronunciation unit of a word, generally made up of a vowel. Monosyllables are words with one syllable such as "Now." Multisyllabic words have more than one syllable such as, "Motor" or "Excitement." Motor has two syllables (mo-tor) and excitement has three (ex-cite-ment).

When people try and show off their vocabulary they often choose big words with lots of syllables. Such as transmogrify (four syllables) or recalcitrant (four syllables). There's nothing inherently wrong with words with many syllables except they take longer for your brain to process and are often unfamiliar. (Also, a lot of people use big words without fully understanding their meaning. But hey, that's another conversation.) The advantage of these words is they can sometimes have a more specific technical meaning. However, video as you'll recall, is not good on detail or technical specifics.

So avoid multisyllables. And understand monosyllables are not about dumbing down an audience. They simply make it easier for your viewer to build their understanding of your message quicker.

Can you replace every multisyllabic word with a monosyllable? Not always. Sometimes you'll need several. So does that fly in the face of my principle of keeping sentences short? Maybe it does. But if it doesn't break the grander principle of making content quicker and easier to understand, then break the "Keep sentences short" rule.

Don't Say:	Instead say:
Perambulate	Wander, amble, walk aimlessly
Commence	Start
Conclude	End
Finalize	Wrap up
Leverage	Take advantage of

When should you use multisyllabic words? When your audience knows what that word means without having to scurry away for a dictionary, or you can't find a more efficient way to express that meaning. For example, "irresponsible" may take too many words to spell out and most people know what it means.

Choose Verbs over Nouns

If you want to make your message slower and more painful for your viewer to piece together, load your sentences with lots of nouns. Consider the following sentence:

- Roger was going to engage in a process of negotiation with his client to find greater savings in production costs.

That sentence burned up twenty-two words. And it wasn't easy to piece together. If we replace the nouns with verbs, we save words and the sentence makes sense:

- Roger negotiated with his client to cut production costs.

When you choose verbs, don't just look for an 'action word.' Search for strong, visual verbs. For example, instead of "Reduce the budget" use, "Cut the budget," instead of "Go," use a word that describe what go means.

Avoid Adverbs

Adverbs work against video scriptwriting. Adverbs are words we use to add a description to other words. Such as walk quickly. They're clumsy and add unnecessary syllables. And they often hide weak nouns and verbs.

Adverbs describe a place, time, level of certainty or degree. You can recognize many adverbs because many end with "ly" such as incredibly, extremely, usually and happily. Of course not every adverb does, such as "Again," "Very" or "Well."

When you find yourself using an adverb, look at the noun or verb you have selected and see if you can't strengthen it first. Stephen King, although talking about writing novels said, "I believe the road to hell is paved with adverbs and I will shout it from the rooftops."

Don't Say:	Instead say:
Walked angrily into the room.	Stormed into the room.
His presentation was perfectly good.	His presentation was good/fine/acceptable.

PART FOUR

PART FOUR – EASY REFERENCE

BUILDING SENTENCES

- Use as few words as you can
- Delete any word you don't need
- Delete tautologies
- Replace conjunctions with a period and start a new sentence
- Avoid adjectives
- Use contractions
- Use simple sentences
- Avoid compound and complex sentences
- Write in the active voice

WORD CHOICE

- Link words to pictures
- Choose simple words
- Lean towards concrete words
- Use monosyllables
- Choose verbs over nouns
- Avoid adverbs

MEDIA WORKSHOPS

Jonathan Halls has taught thousands of people to create engaging digital content around the world. He's taught media professionals in some of the world's leading media houses as well as non-media folks who have found digital content creation to be part of their day-to-day work.

You can attend Jonathan's highly practical public seminars or have him, or one of his colleagues, come in-house to your organization and tailor a class designed to meet your organization's specific needs. They also provide coaching and consulting. Here are some of his most popular media seminars:

- **Video Script Writing Workshop (1-day)**
  Develop the mindset of a video writer and learn techniques to make your information and marketing web videos quick and easy to understand. This workshop is ideal for marketing, corporate communications professionals instructional designers.

- **Video Boot Camp (1-day)**
  Make engaging web video that looks professional using entry-level video cameras. This fast-paced, intensive class which is very popular and lots of fun shows you how to plan, shoot and edit.

- **Intermediate Video Workshop (3-day)**
  Complete video production process. You'll learn to storyboard, write, plan the production, use a camera and edit your footage.

- **Writing for the Web Workshop (2-day)**
  Web browsers read 25% of text they see on a screen. This workshop shows you how to write web text that's engaging on computer screens, tablets and cell phones. Ideal for marketers and corporate communications teams.

Visit **www.JonathanHalls.com** for more information and to get free articles on digital content production.

Made in the USA
San Bernardino, CA
13 August 2019